Bellingrath Gardens
and HOME

A Pictorial Story in Color of the
"Charm Spot of the Deep South"

by

Fred W. Holder

LIBRARY OF CONGRESS CATALOG CARD NUMBER 67-16765 / COPYRIGHT, 1967, BY THE BELLINGRATH-MORSE FOUNDATION

Bellingrath Gardens

There are a few places in the world where magic is still to be found—the magic of beauty so poignant that it fills the heart with awe. Such a place is Bellingrath Gardens, on the Isle-aux-Oies River, near Mobile, Alabama.

Visitors who enter the wrought-iron gates of this vast and lovely estate will soon realize they have come upon a veritable wonderland. Overhead, from branches of aged oaks, trail graceful wisps of Spanish moss. Along the sun-dappled paths the flame of azaleas or the blush of hydrangeas excites the eye with loveliness. An early impression is that of the harmony with which man and nature have combined efforts to produce a magnificent garden. The trail that winds so casually through the whispering pines is frequently enhanced by an artful vista that delightfully blends with the natural surroundings.

One of the happy charms of Bellingrath Gardens is that beauty knows no season here. Mr. Bellingrath was fond of comparing his beloved "Charm Spot of the Deep South" to a lovely lady with 52 gowns, one for each week of the year. The metaphor suggests the constantly changing beauty of the Gardens, ever enchanting, never the same.

From late winter's spectacular azaleas, through springtime's dogwood, roses and hydrangeas, through summer's brilliant foliage plants and flowers, to autumn's exquisite camellias, the pageant moves on, perfumed by Confederate jasmine and sweet olive, sheltered by oak, magnolia, and a variety of other trees.

Literally millions of chrysanthemum flowers in cascades, hanging baskets and mass plantings create a colorful wonder of the world in late fall.

Comments from the many thousands of visitors who tour the Gardens each year are extravagant with praise. Whatever facet of this many-splendored place appeals most to the individual visitor, all share a common experience: the quiet, peaceful and tranquil atmosphere gives one a feeling of reverence and of closer communion with the one Creator of all beauty.

The visitor leaves the entrance building and enters the Gardens through iron gates that once welcomed guests to a Louisiana ante-bellum plantation.

The Rose Garden, planted to resemble the Rotary Club emblem, is in bloom almost nine months of the year.

The Peace rose, with its delicate colors, is a favorite of many visitors.

A bridge of iron lacework and old jumbo handmade brick overlooks the Rose Garden.

Bromeliads, orchids and other exotic plants are on display in the Conservatory.

The Great Lawn, with its broad expanse of green grass, is bordered by a massive display of chrysanthemums and cassias in the late fall.

An azalea tree shows the beauty of its flower against the deep blue of a late winter-early spring sky.

The Biblical story of Rebecca-at-the-Well is depicted on this bronze plaque.

One of many pools which reflect the beauty of the flowers around its borders.

A vista along the mermaid walk during the azalea blooming season.

The mermaid elegantly reigns over her part of the Garden.

An ancient live oak tree, with its hanging Spanish moss, frames this view of cinerarias, Easter lilies and amaryllis.

Another flower-banked pool with fountains playing on the water.

"The flowers appear on the earth; the time of the singing of birds is come . . ." *Song of Solomon 2:12.*

The Christmas season is greeted with the bright colored foliage of the poinsettia.

The trumpet-like
flower of the azalea
has its own
individual beauty...

...or can be
used in mass displays
with other flowers.

The Bellingrath Home, with its mingling of French, English and Mediterranean architecture, houses the Bessie Morse Bellingrath Collection of antiques, priceless silver, fine china and rare porcelains. Visitors in the Home are accompanied by hostesses and/or former servants of the Bellingraths.

The Grotto, with its seasonal plantings, has long been a favorite feature of the Gardens. It is shown at left at azalea time.

In the summertime the golden flower of the allamanda brightens the Grotto ... and in late fall the chrysanthemum is featured.

Small craft from nearby resorts bring guests to this boathouse on the Isle-aux-Oies River.

A view of the
Bellingrath Home
from a walk along
the river.

Beauty,
peace and
tranquility
reign
supreme.

Proud amaryllis stand with their heads held high.

A place to pause on the front
terrace of the Home.

Tropical water lilies star in this pool.

Iron lacework frames a balcony and one of the entrances to the Home.

A Tiger Swallowtail butterf[ly] visits a Lilium rubrum.

Squirrels are happy througho[ut] the Gardens.

Beauty knows no season . . . especially in the Patio of the Bellingrath Home where iron lacework blends with old jumbo handmade brick and seasonal flowers.

This view of the South Terrace and Great Lawn can be enjoyed from the balcony of the Home.

Poinsettias and Easter lilies decorate the Patio near the boy-on-a-dolphin fountain.

The Bellingrath Home

Few residences anywhere combine the charm of design and construction, the richness of furnishings and the rarity of art objects that are to be found in The Bellingrath Home.

The furniture, the old English silver, the fabulous collection of china and rare porcelain are known as The Bessie Morse Bellingrath Collection in memory of Mrs. Bellingrath who painstakingly gathered these priceless objects from all over the world.

The house itself, built in 1935, is of handmade brick and wrought-iron lace work, all over a century old. In the words of the late George B. Rogers, the architect who designed it, the house is "a mingling of the French, English and Mediterranean influences, while the interior represents a blend of decor embracing chiefly the English Renaissance and Colonial America." As handsome as is the exterior of the Home, visitors are still not prepared for the magnificence to be found within.

Here is a comprehensive collection of antique furniture, including French and English pieces that reflect both the Victorian and latter-day French influences. Complementing the furniture are rare 18th and 19th Century pieces of Meissen (Dresden), Sevres and English porcelains. Four different sets of 22-carat gold overlay service plates, one set painted and signed by Angelica Kaufman (c. 1741-1807), are to be seen as well as nine complete dinner services and an exquisite collection of antique silver.

After Mrs. Bellingrath died in 1943, Mr. Bellingrath continued to live in the Home in the center of his beloved Gardens until the time of his death in 1955. It was then opened to the public, according to his wishes, by the non-profit charitable foundation which he had established in 1950.

The Drawing Room of
The Bellingrath Home
includes interesting
period furnishings.

Note the French porcelain
clock and urns by
Jacob Petit, c. 1790,
on the Adam type
mantel. The gold leaf
mirror is Louis XVI.

This priceless Meissen (Dresden) urn, c. 1800, is resplendent in coloring and detail.

The English Chippendale dining table and chairs were once owned by Sir Thomas Lipton. The rare centerpiece is of Meissen porcelain and ormolu.

In the upstairs hall is a hand-carved rosewood console table made for Princess Louise, grandmother of Kaiser Wilhelm II.

This guest bedroom indicates the exquisite detail in which Mrs. Bellingrath furnished the Home.

French porcelain urn (Sevres) c. 1786.

This family group in French bisque, a flawless example of the potter's art, is one of several hundred pieces of bisque and porcelain in the Home.

This hand-carved four-poster
bed is found in the
Purple Room.

Porcelain group (Meissen)
Eighteenth Century.

A corner of the upstairs
"Morning Room".

Mrs. Bellingrath's bedroom in soft pink with touches of blue has a hand-carved bed made by Mallard of Louisiana, c. 1838—

Mr. Bellingrath's bedroom prominently displays this Jacobean style oak desk inlaid in ivory and mother-of-pearl.

This lovely portrait bust
of English bisque by Copeland
has a life-like grace
and softness of contour.

This small dining-room
has many interesting
pieces from
various countries.

A portion of the
China Collection.

The Crystal and Silver Room.

The Bottle Collection is
colorful and unusual.

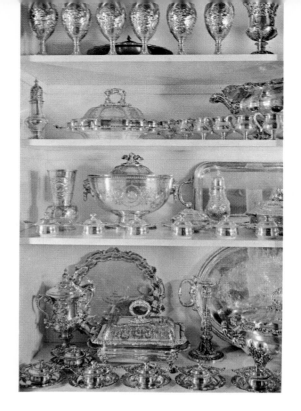

The fabulous collection of old Georgian,
Sheffield and Sterling silver
includes many articles from
the estate of the Earl of Tankerville,
which dates from the 11th Century.

The Alabama marble on the
kitchen table compares with
Italian marble in color and durability.

In the Porch Dining Room hang portraits of Generals Washington, Lee and Jackson done in needle point and petit point.

Visitors are invariably impressed by this table with Honduran mahogany top, Chinese blackwood apron and pedestal base, all hand-carved in a popular Jade pattern.

*A*fter reveling in the works of the finest craftsmen of Europe and America, visitors return to the out-of-doors beauty in Bellingrath Gardens. Having seen so much, it is difficult to believe that still further surprises in loveliness lie ahead. They are soon apparent as visitors stroll along the flagstone paths viewing new vistas and scenes that challenge the imagination.

Daffodils seem to welcome the newborn spring.

Chrysanthemums
are everywhere
in the fall.

Hyacinths bedazzle the spectator in one of many beds.

A collection of Edward Marshall Boehm's sculptures in porcelain was presented to the Gardens by the Delchamps family of Mobile on March 9, 1967. All visitors to the Gardens can enjoy their matchless beauty in the Visitor's Lounge near the Home.

Included in the collection are these wood thrushes and azaleas which seem lifelike.

The song of the song sparrow can almost be heard.

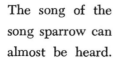

An azalea lined
flagstone walk
leads to the
Summer House.

A view from inside the Summer House.
The walk leads to the Camellia Arboretum
of over nine hundred varieties of camellias.

Nagasaki
Camellia japonica

Dr. Tinsley
Camellia japonica

A graceful swan drifts lazily on Mirror Lake.

This Lilium alba grows
in the sun-dappled shade
of venerable pines and oaks.

The flower of the Rothschild
supreme hybrid azalea is
uniquely colorful.

The vivid reflections in Mirror Lake are responsible for its name.

Swans seem to
enjoy posing
for visitors.

A picturesque setting is created by
the rustic bridge across Mirror Lake.

The deep colors of the
amaryllis are striking.

The Rockery was
created under
Mrs. Bellingrath's
personal supervision.

A begonia nestles
close to a moss
covered stone.

Ferns and the sound of water add
to the charm of the Rockery.

Hydrangeas, aspidistra, nun orchids
and mahonia japonica make a
colorful display in the
late spring.

A Monarch butterfly
matches its brilliant
colors with the
flowers.

The story of the
Gardens is
immortalized in
bronze on this
red granite
Monolith.

Tulips seem to grow naturally in this colorful vista.

The long, sturdy limbs of the live oak trees make a good place for birds to perch and Spanish moss to hang as it gathers nourishment from the air.

Flamingos in the Japanese-American Garden lend their exotic beauty to the area.

The Gardens are a sanctuary for all birds and almost two hundred species either make their homes here or visit during their migrations.

As the walk through
the Gardens nears
an end, it leads
across this bridge
over the Rose Garden.

It is good to pause and contemplate . . . and where can this be done better than in a garden whose only purpose is the reflection of the beauty of God's creation?

WALTER DUNCAN BELLINGRATH
1869-1955

BESSIE MORSE BELLINGRATH
1878-1943

Founders of Bellingrath Gardens

Born in Atlanta, Georgia, Walter D. Bellingrath began his career at the age of 17 as a railroad station agent and telegraph operator for the Louisville and Nashville Railroad in the small Alabama town of Castleberry. At the time of his death at 86, he had become one of the South's great leaders in business, church, educational and civic affairs. He moved to Mobile in 1903 and founded the Coca-Cola Bottling Company there. He later married Bessie Mae Morse of Mobile, whose tireless energy and love of beauty played a predominant part in the masterpiece of their life's work: the creation of Bellingrath Gardens and the establishment of The Bessie Morse Bellingrath Collection of antique furniture, priceless silver, rare porcelains and fine china.

GOD'S GARDEN

THE LORD GOD PLANTED A GARDEN
IN THE FIRST WHITE DAYS OF THE WORLD
AND SET THERE AN ANGEL WARDEN
IN A GARMENT OF LIGHT ENFURLED

SO NEAR TO THE PEACE OF HEAVEN
THE HAWK MIGHT NEST WITH THE WREN
FOR THERE IN THE COOL OF THE EVE'N
GOD WALKED WITH THE FIRST OF MEN

AND I DREAM THAT THESE GARDEN CLOSES
WITH THEIR SHADE AND THEIR SUN-FLECKED SOD
AND THEIR LILIES AND BOWERS OF ROSES
WERE LAID BY THE HAND OF GOD

THE KISS OF THE SUN FOR PARDON
THE SONG OF THE BIRDS FOR MIRTH
ONE IS NEARER GOD'S HEART IN A GARDEN
THAN ANYWHERE ELSE ON EARTH

DOROTHY FRANCES GURNEY

History
OF BELLINGRATH GARDENS

This early painting shows the rustic site of now fabulous Bellingrath Gardens, which began as a fishing lodge for Walter D. and Bessie Morse Bellingrath in 1917. It was Mrs. Bellingrath who first began planting azaleas in the woods around the lodge. So successful were her efforts that she and her husband soon became enthusiastic over the possibility of creating a wondrously beautiful garden from the forest around them.

In 1927, on a trip to Europe, the Bellingraths were enormously impressed by the great gardens they found there. They decided to call upon professional landscape architects to help them in their labor of love on the Isle-aux-Oies River. The aid of George B. Rogers, internationally known landscape designer and architect, was enlisted and the major aspects of the transformation were begun.

Not until 1932 were the Gardens first opened to the public. So overwhelming was the response to the Bellingraths' invitation to come see their gardens that the highway patrol was called to help untangle the traffic snarl. To insure an appreciative audience and to help with the tremendous cost of upkeep, it was decided that an admission fee must be charged. This has been customary ever since.

The Gardens grew in size as additional acres of woodlands surrounding them were landscaped and planted. One of the interesting developments is the Camellia Arboretum, which is intended to provide the camellia enthusiast an opportunity to compare the growing and flowering habits of the many, many varieties of this queen of all flowers. This is perhaps the most complete collection of its kind in the world.

Both Mr. and Mrs. Bellingrath had the satisfaction of seeing their fondest dream become a reality in the unsurpassed beauty of Bellingrath Gardens. Had they been buried in the Gardens instead of in the family plot in Magnolia Cemetery in Mobile, their epitaph might well have been copied from Sir Christopher Wren's in St. Paul's Cathedral, which he designed: "If you seek a monument, look about you."

The Bellingrath-Morse Foundation

The purpose of The Bellingrath-Morse Foundation is best explained in Mr. Bellingrath's own words as written in the preamble to the Deed of Trust creating the Foundation on February 1, 1950.

"In the evening of our lives my beloved wife, Bessie Morse Bellingrath, and I found untold pleasure and happiness in the development of the Gardens which bear our name. During the past decade thousands of our fellow citizens have enjoyed the rare and lovely spectacle which nature, with our help, has provided in this 'Charm Spot of the Deep South.' The inspiration which we received as we carried on our work of developing the Gardens and the pleasant and appreciative reaction of the many visitors to the Gardens resulted in plans for the perpetuation of this beauty, so that those who come after us may visit the Gardens and enjoy them. In working out our plans, it occurred to us that the operation of the Gardens could be carried on in a way that would continue their existence and yet fulfill another worthy objective of ours. To this end, I am providing herein that the income from the operations of the Gardens be devoted to the intellectual and religious upbuilding of young men and women, as well as to foster and perpetuate those Christian values which were recognized by our forefathers as essential for the building of a great nation."

Mr. Bellingrath died on August 8, 1955, leaving the bulk of his estate to the Foundation. Today the Gardens are under the administration of the six trustees of The Bellingrath-Morse Foundation. The Corporate Trustee is the First National Bank of Mobile, of which Mr. Bellingrath was a director. The five individual trustees are men who, over a period of time, were closely associated with Mr. Bellingrath.

With the establishment of The Bellingrath-Morse Foundation, Southwestern at Memphis, Huntingdon College at Montgomery, and Stillman College (for Negroes) at Tuscaloosa became beneficiaries along with the Central Presbyterian Church of Mobile (as a perpetual memorial to his parents), and the St. Francis Street Methodist Church of Mobile (as a perpetual memorial to his wife's parents).

It is incumbent upon the colleges in order to qualify as a beneficiary that each student shall be required to take a course in Bible training. Thus, through the Foundation, Mr. Bellingrath is carrying out a long fostered and cherished plan of perpetuating world famed Bellingrath Gardens and, at the same time, providing long term benefits to the colleges which carry on in the Christian tradition.

Map

1 ENTRANCE GATE

2 ROSE GARDEN
  (Rotary Emblem)

3 BRICK PATIO

4 GREAT LAWN

5 CAMELLIA PARTERRE

6 POOL — REBECCA
  AT THE WELL

7 MONOLITH

8 SOUTH TERRACE

9 GROTTO

10 BOATHOUSE

11 THE BELLINGRATH HOME

12 VISITOR'S LOUNGE
   (REST ROOMS)

13 BAYOU OVERLOOK

14 SUMMER HOUSE

15 CAMELLIA ARBORETUM

16 VIEW ACROSS MIRROR
   LAKE

17 RUSTIC BRIDGE

18 ROCKERY

19 HOLLY GARDENS

20 BRIDGE OVERLOOKING
   ROSE GARDEN

ENTRANCE TO THE
Bellingrath Home

ISLE-AUX-OIES (FOWL) RIVER

NORTH BAYOU

MIRROR LAKE

GROTTO

GREAT LAWN

CAMELLIA ARBORETUM

BELLINGRATH HOME

PET MOTEL

PARKING AREA

ENTRANCE BUILDING
Restaurant, Gift Shop
& Lounges

Bellingrath Gardens
and HOME

LITHO-KROME® U.S.A.
COLUMBUS, GEORGIA